Off to the Forest

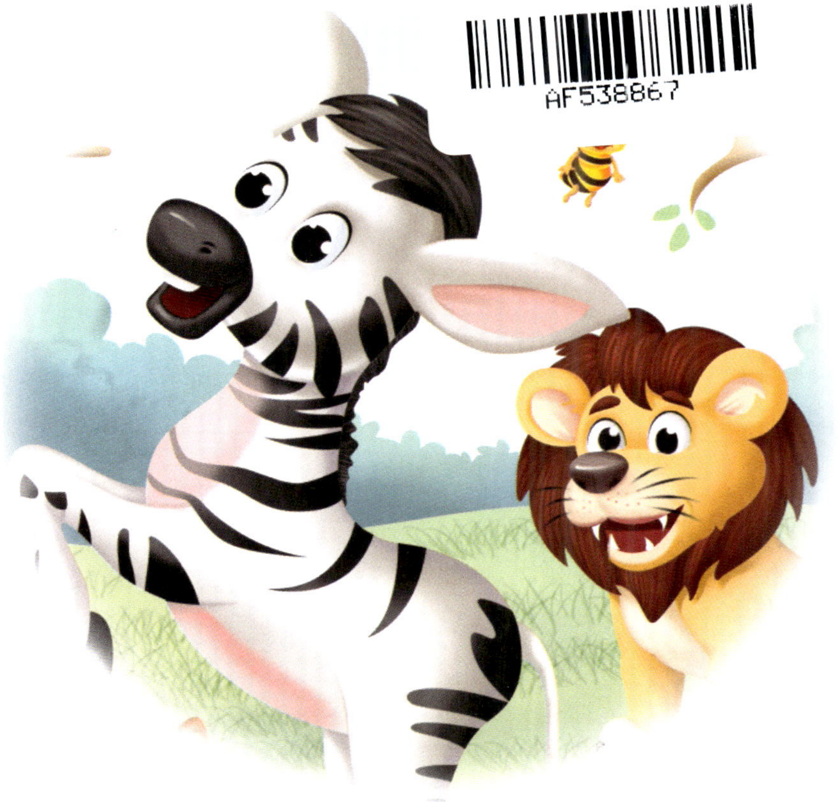

Om KIDZ
An imprint of Om Books International

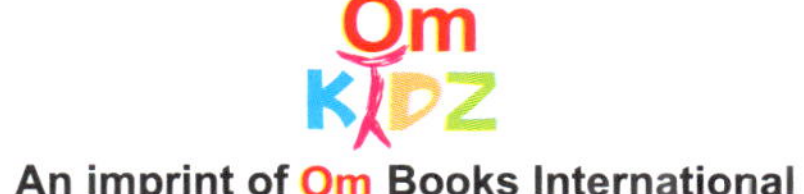

Reprinted in 2025

Corporate & Editorial Office
A-12, Sector 64, Noida 201 301
Uttar Pradesh, India
Phone: +91 120 477 4100
Email: editorial@ombooks.com
Website: www.ombooksinternational.com

Sales Office
107, Ansari Road, Darya Ganj
New Delhi 110 002, India
Phone: +91 11 4000 9000
Email: sales@ombooks.com
Website: www.ombooks.com

ISBN: 978-93-86108-89-0

Printed in India

10 9 8 7 6 5 4 3

Off to the Forest

I'm all set to read

Paste your photograph here

My name is

Zee, the Zebra is **sad**.

Her stripes **are** lost. **She** looks funny without **her** stripes.

Bip, the bee comes buzzing along. "**Zee**, where **are** your stripes?" **she** asks.

"I have lost them," says **Zee**. "**Can you see** them anywhere?"

Ola, the owl comes hooting. "**Zee**, where **are** your stripes?" **she** asks. "I have lost them," says **Zee**. "Please help me find them."

Leo, **the** lion looks **out** from **his den**. “**Zee**, **you** look **odd** without your stripes. Where **are** they?”

“I have lost them,” says **Zee**. “Please help me find them.”

Amo, the ant comes crawling up.

"**Zee**, your stripes **are** gone.

Where **are** they?"

"I have lost them," says **Zee**.

"Please help me find them."

The animals think hard. Where **can the** stripes be? They **hop** around to **see**. They look under **the log**. They look under **the fig** tree.

Just then **Flo, the sly fox** comes there. "What **are you all** looking **for**?" **she** asks.

"We **are** looking **for Zee**'s stripes," **the** animals **say**.

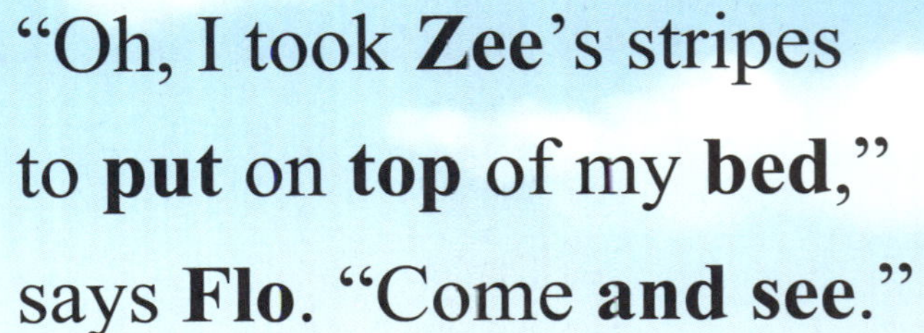

“Oh, I took **Zee**’s stripes
to **put** on **top** of my **bed**,”
says **Flo**. “Come **and see**.”

The animals **all** go **off** to **Flo**'s house. They **see the** stripes on **Flo**'s **bed**. **The** stripes make **the bed** look so nice.

"**You can**'t take **Zee**'s stripes like that, **Flo**," says **Leo the** lion. "It is **not** right to take someone's things without asking them."

The animals take **the** stripes back to **Zee**. **Zee** is about to **eat** some grass. **She** is still **sad**.

“Look what we have **for you**, **Zee**,” **Bip the bee** says.

They **put the** stripes back on **top** of **Zee**. **Now Zee** is happy again. **She** is looking nice. **She** begins to **hop** around with **joy**.

"I am sorry **Zee, for** taking your stripes," **Flo** says.

"That is **all** right. **Let** us have some **fun now**," says **Zee**, giving **Flo** a **hug**.

Unscramble the word that goes with each picture.

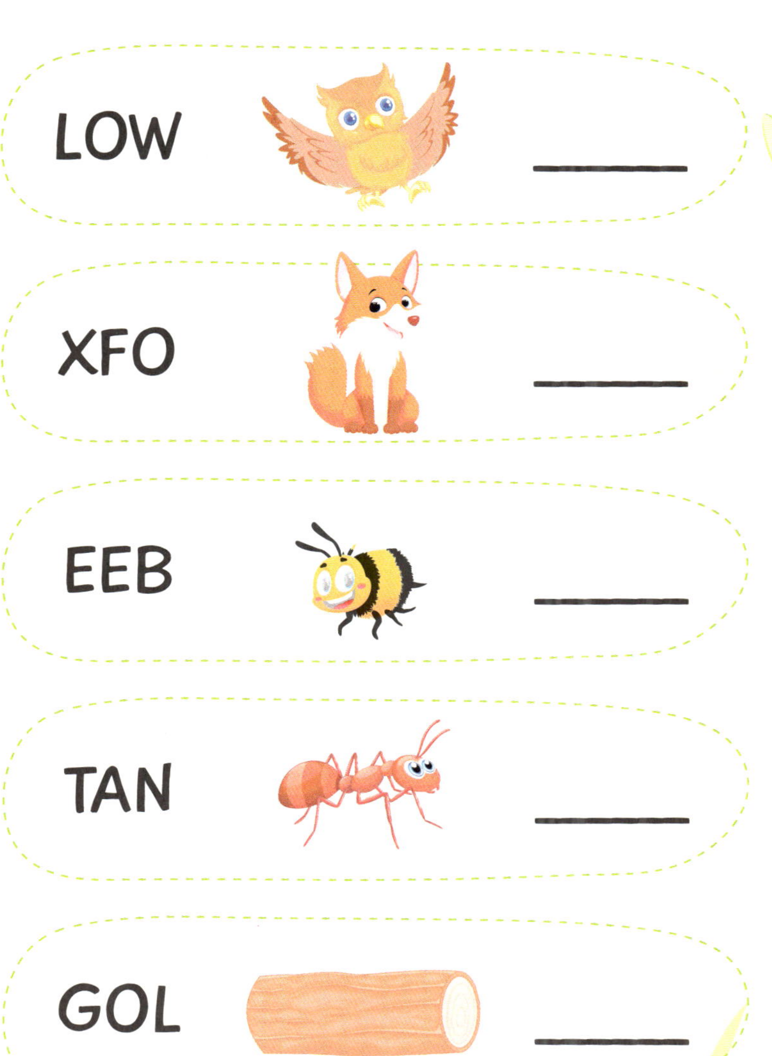

Write words that rhyme.

SEE – ________

LOG – ________

ANT – ________

FOX – ________

TOP – ________

BED – ________

Find the three-letter words hidden in the words given below.

L E T T E R

P A N T

C A N E

S T O P

S E A T

T A L L

Know your words

Sight Words

sad	out	off	she
the	his	not	can
her	odd	joy	for
are	sly	let	and
you	all	now	fun

Naming Words

Zee	owl	ant	fox
Bip	Leo	log	top
bee	den	fig	bed
Ola	Amo	Flo	

Doing Words

see	put	hop
say	eat	hug